Pedal Power

Lisa James

Photography by Russell Millard

Look at the **pedal**. You make a pedal work by pushing down on it with your foot.

The pedal is joined to a **chain**.

When you push down on the pedal, it makes the chain move.

The chain has little **links**. The links lock onto the **cogs** of a wheel and turn it.

A cog has small **teeth** around its edge. These catch the chain.

As the chain moves around, it moves the cog around, too.

This is an **axle**. The axle goes through the middle of the cogs and the wheel.

The axle makes the wheel turn.

This is a steering **lever**. A steering lever is joined to the wheels on the ground.

When you pull on the steering lever, the wheels turn.

The steering lever joins to these parts, and makes the wheels turn.

If you pull the steering lever to the left, you will go to the left. If you pull the steering lever to the right, you will go to the right.

This is a **screw.** A screw is turned by a **screwdriver**.

The grooves on a screw are called the **thread**.

The thread makes the screw very strong at holding things together.

This screw holds things in place.

Brakes slow things down. The brake has a **cable.** The cable joins a brake hand lever to a **clamp** on the wheel.

If you pull the brake hand lever, it pulls the cable. Then, the clamp will touch the wheel. This slows the wheel down.

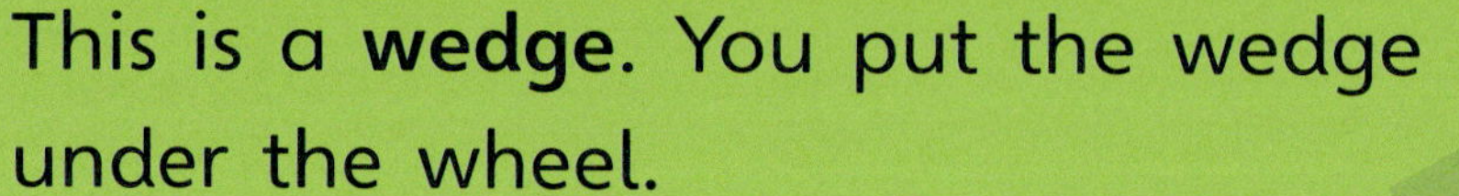

This is a **wedge**. You put the wedge under the wheel.

The wedge will stop the wheel from moving.

This is a **helmet**. A helmet helps keep you safe.

If you hit your head, the helmet gets damaged, not your head!

This is a **hinge**. Hinges let you open things.

A hinge lets you open this top.
The top is called a **canopy**.

This is a **pedal car**!

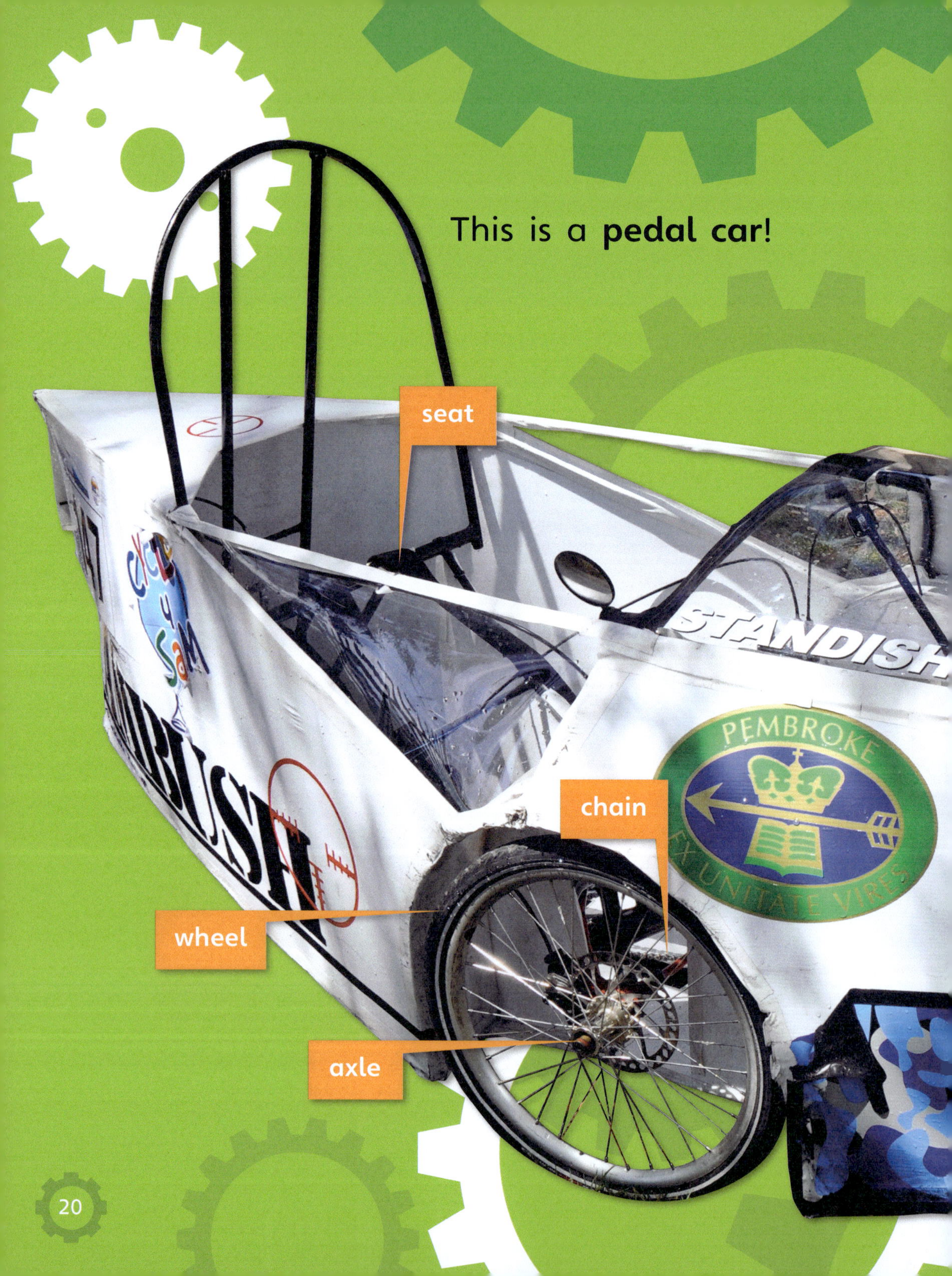

Pedal cars move when you push down on the pedals.

The pedal moves the chain.

The chain moves the cog.

The cog moves the axle.

The axle moves the wheel.

This is a pedal car race!

147
AMBUSH
ROAD HAZARD
woodhead
Cycle 4 SaM
Flying Cougars
STANDISH
coles
153
COMPLETE
Ute and Van Hire
8244 5333
PACHYDERM

Glossary

axle	the rod through the middle of a wheel
cable	a strong rope of twisted wire
canopy	a cover that acts like a roof
chain	a row of rings or links joined together
clamp	this holds things together
cogs	bits sticking out from a wheel that allow it to turn another wheel or a chain
helmet	a strong cover to protect your head
hinge	something that holds two things together so they can swing open or closed
lever	a bar that is pushed or pulled to make a machine work
links	pieces of a chain
pedal	a part of a machine that is pushed by a person's foot
pedal car	a car that moves when you push on its pedals
screw	a metal pin with grooves around it
screwdriver	a tool for turning screws
teeth	the pointed bits on a cog
thread	the grooves on a screw
wedge	a block of wood used to stop an object from sliding or rolling